For Walter and Molly

—————

FOREWORD

When my children were very young we sorted my collection of fine art postcards into numerous categories—happy pictures, sad pictures, noisy pictures, pictures with dogs or doves or cats or funny hats. We filled a large photo album, in which each spread represented a letter of the alphabet, that eventually became my first art book, *I Spy: An Alphabet in Art*.

I realized early on that my children were learning a great deal simply by looking. They didn't know the names of the artists, but they could recognize the wonky eyes in a Picasso or the quality of light in a Caravaggio. We talked about the paintings as if they were ordinary pictures in a picture book, finding funny details, colors, shapes; but also we found myths and legends, Bible stories, scenes from all over the world and throughout history. It occurred to me then that if every child in every home and every classroom could be introduced to art (by means of just a few paintings), then they would all grow up with access to this amazing source of knowledge and inspiration.

My children, now grown-up, have helped me to choose the pictures for *I Spy Colors in Art*. There's plenty to talk about. As well as the colors, there are shapes to find and elephants to count; there is a hairy caterpillar, a young boy in a dress, a boiled egg for breakfast, and, of course, some of Picasso's wonky eyes.

Lucy Micklethwait, 2007

I Spy
Colors in Art

Devised & selected by Lucy Micklethwait

Greenwillow Books
An Imprint of HarperCollins*Publishers*

I spy
with my little eye

a red key

Michael Craig-Martin, *Untitled*

I spy
with my little eye

a yellow
circle

Robert Delaunay, *Rhythm No.1*

I spy
with my little eye

two
blue eyes

Pablo Picasso, *Maya with a Doll*

I spy
with my little eye

an orange
orange

John Frederick Peto, *The Poor Man's Store*

I spy
with my little eye

a purple
square

Richard Paul Lohse, *Movement Around a Foursquared Center*

I spy
with my little eye

a green
elephant

The fabulous region of Himavant, from a Burmese manuscript

I spy
with my little eye

gray smoke

Ando Hiroshige, *Fuji from the Sagami River*

I spy
with my little eye

a pair of
pink socks

Peter Blake, *On the Balcony*

I spy
with my little eye

a black
beetle

Jan van Kessel, *Insects*

I spy
with my little eye

a white
moon

René Magritte, *Le Maître d'Ecole*

I spy
with my little eye

a brown
cow

The Nativity, from a French Book of Hours (15th century)

I spy
with my little eye

a silver
spoon

Bernhard Dörries, *Breakfast Still Life*

I spy
with my little eye

a gold bell

Diego Velázquez, *Prince Felipe Próspero*

I spy
with my little eye

lots of colors

*How many colors
can you spy?*

Michael Craig-Martin, *Eye Test*

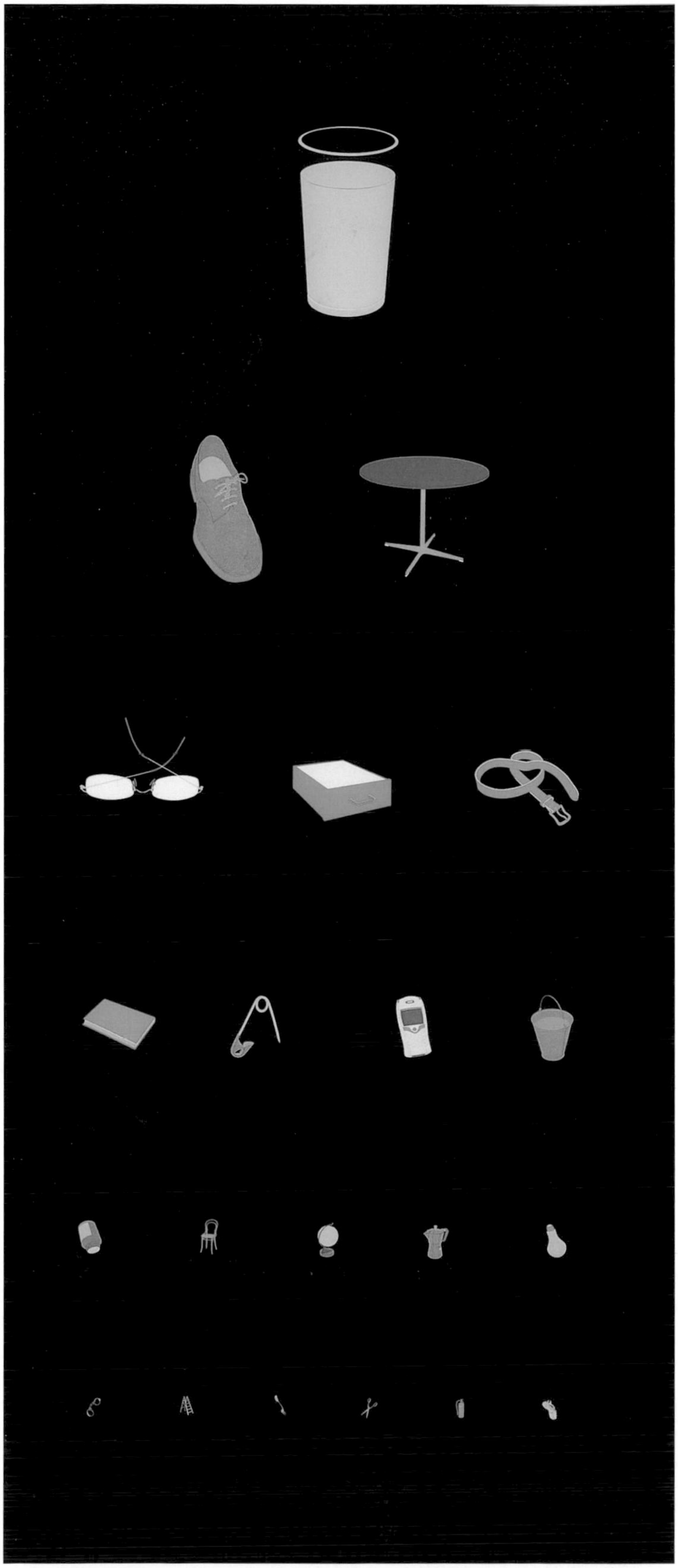

I Spied with My Little Eye

Red
Michael Craig-Martin (born 1941), *Untitled* (1998)
Government Art Collection, London

Yellow
Robert Delaunay (1885–1941), *Rhythm No.1* (1938)
Museé National d'Art Moderne, Centre Georges Pompidou, Paris

Blue
Pablo Picasso (1881–1973), *Maya with a Doll* (1938)
Museé Picasso, Paris

Orange
John Frederick Peto (1854–1907), *The Poor Man's Store* (1885)
Museum of Fine Arts, Boston

Purple
Richard Paul Lohse (1902–1988), *Movement Around a Foursquared Center* (1958–1969)
Kunstmuseum, Winterthur

Green
The fabulous region of Himavant, from a Burmese manuscript (19th century)
The British Library, London

Gray
Ando Hiroshige (1797–1858), *Fuji from the Sagami River,* from the

series *Thirty-six Views of Fuji* (c. 1858)
The Newark Museum, John Cotton Dana Collection

Pink
Peter Blake (born 1932), *On the Balcony* (1955-1957)
Tate Gallery, London

Black
Jan van Kessel (1626-1679), *Insects* (date unknown)
The Fitzwilliam Museum, Cambridge, England

White
René Magritte (1898-1967), *Le Maître d'Ecole* (1955)
Private Collection

Brown
The Nativity, from a French Book of Hours (15th century)
The Fitzwilliam Museum, Cambridge, England

Silver
Bernhard Dörries (1898-1978), *Breakfast Still Life* (1927)
Sprengel Museum, Hanover

Gold
Diego Velázquez (1599-1660), *Prince Felipe Próspero* (1659)
Kunsthistorisches Museum, Vienna

Lots of colors
Michael Craig-Martin (born 1941), *Eye Test* (2005)
Private Collection

ACKNOWLEDGMENTS

The author and publishers would like to thank the galleries, museums, private collectors, and copyright holders who have given their permission to reproduce the pictures in this book.

Michael Craig-Martin, *Untitled*: Inv. Nr 17319,
Courtesy of the Government Art Collection (UK) © Michael Craig-Martin and Gagosian Gallery

Robert Delaunay, *Rhythm No. 1*: inside and cover, © L&M Services B.V. Amsterdam 20060808

Pablo Picasso, *Maya with a doll*: © Photo RMN/© Jean-Gilles Berizzi. © Succession Picasso/ DACS 2007. HarperCollins has paid DACS' visual creators for the use of their artistic works

John Frederick Peto, *The Poor Man's Store*: Gift of Maxim Karolik for the M. and M. Karolik Collection of American Paintings, 1815-1865 62.278.
Photograph © 2007 Museum of Fine Arts, Boston

Richard Paul Lohse, *Movement Around a Foursquared Center*: inside and frontis,
Kunstmuseum Winterthur. Purchase, 1972.
© DACS 2007. HarperCollins has paid DACS' visual creators for the use of their artistic works

The fabulous region of Himavant, from a Burmese manuscript: Burmese Buddhist Cosmology/ The British Library, London Or. 14004, f.34 © The British Library, London

Ando Hiroshige, *Fuji from the Sagami River*: Work Collection of The Newark Museum,
John Cotton Dana Collection. Inv: 00.117. Newark, The Newark Museum.
© Photo The Newark Museum/Art Resource/Scala, London

Peter Blake, *On the Balcony*: © TATE, London 2006. © Peter Blake.
Licensed by DACS 2007. HarperCollins has paid DACS' visual creators for the use of their artistic works

Jan van Kessel 1, *Insects*: Accession Number 309. Reproduction by permission of the Syndics of The Fitzwilliam Museum, Cambridge

René Magritte, *Le Maître d'Ecole*: © Photothèque R. Magritte - ADAGP, Paris 2006.
© ADAGP, Paris and DACS, London 2007.
HarperCollins has paid DACS' visual creators for the use of their artistic works

The Nativity, from a French Book of Hours: MS 69. folio 48 recto.
Reproduction by permission of the Syndics of The Fitzwilliam Museum, Cambridge

Bernhard Dörries, *Breakfast Still Life*: Sprengel Museum, Hanover, Germany. Oil on board.
Dimensions: 51.2 x 69.8. © DACS 2007. HarperCollins has paid DACS' visual creators for the use of their artistic works

Diego Velázquez, *Prince Felipe Próspero*: Kunsthistorisches Museum, Vienna

Michael Craig-Martin, *Eye Test*: Reproduced courtesy of the artist and Alan Cristea Gallery

I Spy Colors in Art

Compilation and text copyright © 2007 by Lucy Micklethwait

First published in 2007 in Great Britain by Collins Picture Books.

First published in 2007 in the United States by Greenwillow Books.

The text type is Galahad Regular.

Library of Congress Cataloging-in Publication Data

Micklethwait, Lucy.

I spy colors in art / devised & selected by Lucy Micklethwait.

 p. cm.

"Greenwillow Books."

ISBN-13: 978-0-06-134837-2 ISBN-10: 0-06-134837-6

[1. Color in art—Juvenile literature. 2. Painting—Juvenile literature.]

I. Title. II. Title: Colors in art.

ND1490.M53 2007 752 —dc22 2006036552

First American Edition 10 9 8 7 6 5 4 3 2 1

Greenwillow Books

Cover picture: Robert Delaunay, *Rhythm No. 1*

Title page picture: Richard Paul Lohse, *Movement Around a Foursquared Center*